WORLD WATCH

GREENPEACE

Sean Sheehan

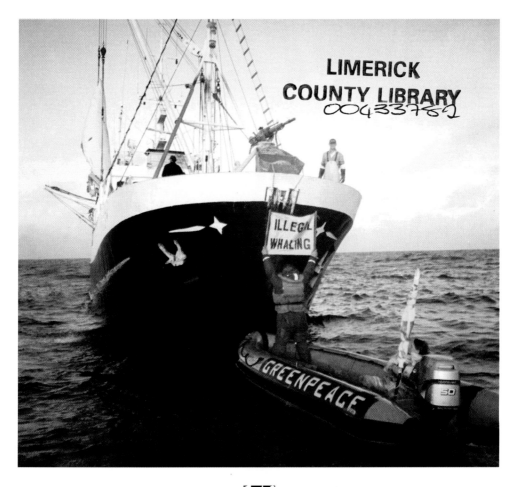

HODDER
Wayland

an imprint of Hodder Children's Books

WORLDWATCH SERIES

Greenpeace • WWF • Red Cross •
World Health Organization • United Nations • UNICEF

Published for Hodder Wayland by White-Thomson Publishing Ltd,
2/3 St Andrew's Place, Lewes, East Sussex BN7 1UP

 © White-Thomson Publishing

Published in Great Britain in 2003 by Hodder Wayland, an imprint of Hodder Children's
Books

Project editor: Andrew Solway
Commissioning editor: Steve White-Thomson
Proofreader: Joanna Harris
Design: Jane Hawkins

British Library Cataloguing in Publication Data
Sheehan, Sean, 1951-
  Greenpeace. - (Worldwatch)
  1. Greenpeace - Juvenile literature
  I. Title II. Solway, Andrew
  363.7'0526

ISBN 0 7502 4187 X

Printed in Hong Kong

Hodder Children's Books, a division of Hodder Headline Ltd,
338 Euston Road, London NW1 3BH.

Picture acknowledgements:
Greenpeace cover, 4, 6 (Kezlere), 8 (Beltra), 10, 11, 12, 13, 15, 17 (Morgan), 18, 19, 21, 22, 23, 24,
26, 27, 28 (Sims), 30, 31, 34, 35, 36, 37, 38, 39, 40, 41, 42, 43, 45 (Morgan); Popperfoto 32 (Steve
Morgan), 33, 44 (Loren Callahan); Still Pictures 5 (Thomas D. Mangelson), 14 (Hartmut Schwarz),
16 (Pasal Kobeh), 20 (Ray Pfortner).
Cover: Rainbow Warrior, Cherbourg.

Disclaimer:
The website addresses (URLs) included in this book were valid at the time of going to press.
However, because of the nature of the Internet, it is possible that some addresses may have changed,
or sites may have changed or closed down since publication. While the author, packager and
publisher regret any inconvenience that this may cause readers, no responsibility for any such
changes can be accepted by either the author, the packager or the publisher.

CONTENTS

Chapter One:
Greenpeace is Born

On a calm September afternoon in 1971, an ancient 80-foot fishing boat and its inexperienced crew set out from Vancouver, Canada, into the North Pacific Ocean. The boat was called the *Phyllis Cormack*, but it was later renamed *Greenpeace*. The voyage was the beginning of what would become the world's largest environmental campaigning group.

AGAINST NUCLEAR TESTING

The aim of the voyage was to draw the public's attention to US plans to explode a nuclear bomb underground on Amchitka Island, a nature reserve in the Aleutian Islands, near Alaska. The crew were Canadians, and this meant that US vessels protecting the detonation site could not stop and arrest them in international waters. But the US government was determined to prevent any interference with the testing of their newest nuclear weapon.

TELLING THE WORLD

The waters of the North Pacific are often treacherous, and only a couple of the crew had ever been to sea before. For most of the crew, cameras and radios were their most important equipment. They planned to record the nuclear test, and send out pictures and reports to the Canadian and American public. The island stood on an active earthquake belt, and many Americans and Canadians were anxious that the nuclear explosion might trigger an earth tremor.

Greenpeace campaigner Dave Birmingham raises the sail of the *Phyllis Cormack* during the voyage to Amchitka Island. ▼

A SUCCESSFUL CAMPAIGN

In the event, the Greenpeace boat didn't make it to Amchitka. Fierce storms forced the crew to shelter in a port on the Aleutian Islands. This gave the US Coast Guard an excuse to arrest the crew, on the little-used charge of failing to clear customs. The nuclear test went ahead, but the voyage had attracted enormous media attention, and the world was made aware that such tests were taking place. Soon afterwards, the US

▲ The Aleutian Islands are home to endangered species such as the bald eagle.

announced that it would no longer be using the Aleutian Islands as a nuclear testing site.

ORGANIZATION IN FOCUS

Founded: 1971

Headquarters: Greenpeace International, Keizersgracht 176, 1016 DW Amsterdam, The Netherlands

Website: www.greenpeace.org (in the UK, www.greenpeace.org.uk)

Structure: Greenpeace is a non-governmental organization (NGO) – an organization that does not seek to make a profit and is not connected with any government. It has offices in 39 countries worldwide. The various national offices are run independently of Greenpeace International.

Funding: Financed by contributions from people who join Greenpeace and by donations from members of the public.

Membership: Worldwide there are around $2^1/_2$ million individual members.

Chapter Two:
The History of Greenpeace

Greenpeace was founded in a church in Vancouver in 1970. It was here that the people who later became the crew of the *Phyllis Cormack* first got together. The founding members raised the money to hire the *Phyllis Cormack* from concerts and donations. At the end of their campaign they had valuable experience of how to use the media (newspapers, television and radio) to promote their cause, how to take direct action, and a kitty of $9000.

THE GREENPEACE FOUNDATION

Once the group's original objective of stopping nuclear testing in the Aleutians had been achieved, some of the founding members left Greenpeace and moved on to other things. Other members of the original group wanted to keep things going. They formed the Greenpeace Foundation, with Ben Metcalfe, a radio journalist and an experienced Canadian politician, as the chairman.

GREEN PEACE

The protesters chose the name Greenpeace because it seemed to sum up what they were campaigning for – 'green' because they were aiming to protect the environment, and 'peace' because they were committed to peaceful protest. Outside of the Canadian group, in countries such as the US and the UK, other groups formed with similar aims, loosely linked with the Vancouver Greenpeace Foundation.

Some of Greenpeace's founder members, from left to right Robert Hunter, Patrick Moore, Bob Cummings, Ben Metcalf and Dave Birmingham. ▼

ORGANIZATION IN FOCUS:
Greenpeace's primary aims

The original Greenpeace group wanted to bring public attention to the American use of the Aleutian Islands as a nuclear test site. From this simple aim, Greenpeace's aims have developed to include the following:

• To protect the climate and ozone layer by ensuring that governments of industrialized countries reduce emissions of greenhouse and ozone-depleting gases;

• To prevent overfishing, pollution, and dumping of waste and other hazardous substances in the sea;

• To change refrigeration and air-conditioning in order to stop the use of ozone-depleting chemicals;

• To monitor and ensure enforcement of global controls on the international waste trade;

• To protect ancient forests, and to promote economic alternatives to intensive logging;

• To eliminate the use of hazardous chemicals (in particular chlorine, which is still used widely for paper bleaching, PVC, and other industrial uses in spite of mounting evidence of their damage to human and animal health);

• To stop commercial whaling;

• To halt the nuclear threat;

• To stop the spread of genetically modified organisms in the natural environment.

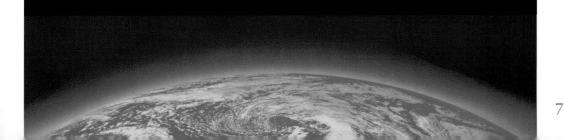

HITTING THE HEADLINES

Encouraged by their success in halting American nuclear testing in the Aleutians, Greenpeace turned its attention to other areas. France, another nuclear power, was also testing nuclear bombs, this time not under the ground but in the open atmosphere on Moruroa Atoll, part of the French Polynesian Islands in the South Pacific. Greenpeace ships such as the *Vega*, the *Magic Isle* and *The Boy* sailed out to the test site to try to prevent the tests taking place. They were harassed by French Navy vessels, and the *Vega* was rammed and damaged. By 1973 Greenpeace's actions had raised a storm of protest, and both the Australian and New Zealand governments sent their own warships to the area to protest at the testing. After an unpleasant scene on the high seas, when Greenpeace protestors were attacked and injured by French commandos, France announced in 1974 that all further nuclear tests would take place underground.

WHALES AND SEALS

From nuclear testing Greenpeace turned its attention to whaling and the culling of seals for their fur. In 1975, small Greenpeace boats were used to confront Russian whaling ships, shielding whales from the harpoon guns. In 1976 Greenpeace began a campaign against the culling of seal pups in Newfoundland, Canada. And in 1978 the *Rainbow Warrior*, Greenpeace's flagship, was brought into service against Norwegian whaling ships in an effort to get an international ban on whaling.

French commandos board a Greenpeace ship near Moruroa in the Pacific Ocean, during Greenpeace's protests against French testing of nuclear weapons. ▼

MORE CAMPAIGNS

From these early campaigns, Greenpeace went on to highlight the dangers of dumping nuclear waste, pollution, and other activities that caused damage to the environment.

In the 1980s Greenpeace began efforts to protect Antarctica as a world park. By this time, it was an international organization with millions of members, and world governments paid attention to its protests.

FACTFILE: Greenpeace Campaigns, 1970s and 1980s

1971 The *Phyllis Cormack* sails to the Aleutian Islands.

1972 US government abandons nuclear testing in Aleutian Islands.

1973 Crew members of the *Vega* are attacked by French navy commandos in the South Pacific.

1974 France abandons surface nuclear testing.

1975 Greenpeace turns its attention to commercial whaling ships.

1976 Greenpeace launches an expedition to prevent the massacre of hundreds of seal pups in Newfoundland. 'Active membership' of the organization reaches 8,000.

1978 The *Rainbow Warrior* is named and joins the anti-whaling protests.

Greenpeace exposes the dumping of nuclear waste at sea by the British and French governments.

1981 Two new ships, *Sirius* and *Cederlea*, join the Greenpeace fleet.

1982 The International Whaling Commission (IWC) votes, by 25 to seven, to end all commercial whaling in three years' time.

1985 French secret service agents bomb Greenpeace's ship *Rainbow Warrior* in Auckland, New Zealand.

1987 Iceland announces that it is ending 'scientific whaling'.

1988 Sixty-five countries decide to halt all ocean incineration of toxic (poisonous) waste by the end of 1994.

1989 *MV Greenpeace* succeeds in halting the testing of the Trident II nuclear missile off the coast of Florida.

WHO RUNS GREENPEACE?

By the late 1970s Greenpeace had offices in the USA, Canada and Europe. The various offices were linked only by informal ties and this sometimes made co-ordinating their campaigns and activities difficult. It became obvious that it was time to organize differently.

In 1979 Greenpeace International (GPI) was formed with its headquarters in Holland. The first Executive Director (head) of GPI was David McTaggart, a veteran sailor and campaigner from the 1972 Moruroa campaign, and a successful businessman. GPI's current Executive Director is Dr Gerd Leipold. He took charge in 2001.

GPI is at the centre of a closely-knit network of national and regional offices. The national offices receive donations and contributions from over 2½ million supporters, and in turn they fund Greenpeace International. Most national offices contribute about a fifth of their income to support GPI and the large fleet of Greenpeace ships.

Greenpeace International and the Greenpeace national offices have an annual meeting to decide which campaigns they should focus on in the next year. Once a campaign has been chosen, it is the job of the GPI

David McTaggart was the first Director of Greenpeace International. This photo of him was taken on board the yacht *Vega* in 1981, during another protest against French nuclear tests. ▼

Campaigns Director to decide how it should be run. He or she may assign one of GPI's fleet to a particular part of the campaign. National offices have one or two campaigns that are particularly relevant for them, which they work on independently of Greenpeace International. For instance Greenpeace UK is campaigning against the use of polluting incinerators to burn rubbish, while Greenpeace Canada is campaigning to save ancient forests, which contain many irreplaceable species of animals and plants.

Once a campaign is under way, Greenpeace International goes into action very much like any international company. The Financial Co-ordinator decides how much

▲ A Greenpeace campaigner climbs a cooling tower at a nuclear power plant near Koblenz, Germany, in 1993. Campaigners hung up a large banner reading 'shutdown instead of startup'. They were protesting against plans to reopen the power station, which had been closed since 1988.

money the campaign will need, and the personnel office finds the people to work on it. The Campaigns Director oversees the running of the campaign, and the Communications Director makes sure that the press and other groups are kept informed about the campaign's progress. Each national organization has a similar group of full-time employees to campaign and raise funds in that country.

GETTING FINANCED

In the last ten years Greenpeace has raised its funds almost entirely from money given by the public. In the past, money was raised by street collections and by selling merchandise (things like badges and T-shirts), but today the organization focuses on long-term supporters – people who regularly contribute small amounts of money, rather than making one-off donations. In many countries, such as the UK, Greenpeace is not registered as a charity, because charities have to avoid any political activity. In other countries such as Canada, the government has taken away Greenpeace's charitable status.

We have seen that most national Greenpeace organizations fund not only themselves but also GPI. However, in poorer countries or countries where a new Greenpeace organization is setting up, GPI provides the funds for the organization.

Greenpeace recruits employees for their skills in such areas as personnel, sales and communications, as well as for their commitment to the Greenpeace cause. The current Chair of the GPI Board of Directors, for instance, was previously the editor of a women's magazine. However most Greenpeace workers are not paid employees but unpaid activists. They take part in campaigns, run the offices, deliver leaflets and ask the opinions of people on the streets.

In the 1990s Greenpeace membership fell from its peak of over

Rebecca Lerer is a Greenpeace worker in the Greenpeace Amazon office in Manaus, Brazil. Her job is to get Greenpeace stories into local newspapers and on TV and radio. ▶

5 million to about half this, probably as part of a general loss of interest in environmental concerns since the mid-1980s. As the number of members fell, Greenpeace's income fell, too.

In recent years the organization has cut spending on administration and has begun to reverse the decline in membership.

Greenpeace volunteers do still sometimes make street collections. This volunteer is collecting outside a supermarket in London, UK. ▶

FACTFILE: Activists or managers?

One criticism that has been levelled at Greenpeace is that it is no longer run by activists who are involved directly in Greenpeace campaigns, but by well-paid businesspeople who run the organization like a profit-making company. In 1996, on Greenpeace's 25th anniversary, fifteen of the founder members of Greenpeace, including the first GPI director David McTaggart, wrote to the organization to make this point.

Another founder member who later left Greenpeace, Paul Watson, makes a different criticism. He thinks that Greenpeace takes money and publicity away from smaller campaigning groups and inadvertently discourages activism. "People don't get involved individually because they think by giving a few hundred bucks a year to Greenpeace, they help save the environment."

THE GLOBAL ENVIRONMENT

Greenpeace's major campaigns are all concerned with stopping the damage that human beings are doing to the planet. We burn up fossil fuels such as coal and oil, which pollute the air and cause global warming. We cut down ancient forests for their wood and to clear the land, without concern for the thousands of animals and plants that no longer have a place to live.

Not only that, but we dump poisons into the sea and catch too many fish. We have allowed natural wildernesses to be mined for profit. We develop new technologies such as genetically modified crops without knowing what effects they might have on the natural environment.

GLOBAL WARMING

Global warming is a serious threat to the future of most life on the planet. For centuries, people have been burning fossil fuels such as coal and oil. When they burn, these fuels release carbon dioxide and other gases into the atmosphere. Scientists think that the increased amount of these gases traps more of the Sun's heat, which makes the Earth heat up. This trapping of heat is known as the greenhouse effect.

As a result of the greenhouse effect, the ice at the North and South Poles has begun to melt, raising sea levels and affecting the world's climate.

Exhaust gases from cars are a major cause of global warming. ▼

THE OZONE HOLE

Other gases called CFCs, which were until recently used in aerosols and refrigerators, have also damaged the Earth's atmosphere. They have begun to destroy a layer of the Earth's atmosphere known as the ozone layer. The ozone layer prevents large amounts of harmful ultraviolet radiation from reaching the Earth's surface. With the ozone layer damaged, far more ultraviolet radiation now reaches the surface.

GREENPEACE'S CONCERNS

As we burn the Earth's fossil fuels, cut down swathes of forest and dump unwanted poisons into the seas, we are in danger of destroying the planet's ability to heal itself. Greenpeace campaigns to make governments pass laws to control the damage we are doing to the planet. It also seeks to find other ways of doing things that do not damage the environment.

▲ More than half the world's animal and plant species are found in rainforests. Logging of the rainforest is driving many of these forest species towards extinction.

"I spent 10 months in Vancouver last year working on the Great Bear Rainforest campaign. We succeeded in protecting 20 valleys from logging completely and another 68 valleys went into a 2-year moratorium [will not be logged for 2 years]. The coolest thing was when I did a walk with my colleagues into the Elaho Valley not far from Vancouver ... I was able to walk through this stunning untouched area knowing that Greenpeace had helped stop it getting completely destroyed."

Tim, a British campaigner

THE ANIMAL WORLD

Not only is the planet itself
threatened by human actions but so
too are the other creatures that live
on it. Many species have already
become extinct, and many more are
on international lists of endangered
animals, whose numbers are so small
that they may soon die out.

Threats to species

The destruction of forests and other
habitats on land, and overfishing in
the oceans, are two of the main
reasons that so many species are
threatened. Global warming is also a
major threat. It could wipe out whole
groups of plants and animals, because
living things in a particular
environment depend on one another
for survival. Plant-eating animals
depend on the plants for food, while
carnivorous animals feed on the
plant-eaters. The plants in their turn
depend on insects and other animals
to carry pollen from flower to flower,
and to carry their seeds to new areas.

▲ Dead white corals on a reef in the Maldives,
south of India. Such damage to coral reefs is
caused by global warming.

If one type of animal or plant dies
because of climate change then all the
other life forms that depend on it may
also die out.

Sea otter collapse

In the Aleutian Islands, where
Greenpeace fought its first anti-
nuclear campaign, there has been a
drastic drop in the number of sea
otters. The causes of this drop and its
effects show how damage to one
species can affect a whole ecosystem.
Scientists think that killer whales have
been eating the sea otters, because the
whales' usual food (sea lions) has
almost disappeared. Sea lion numbers
dropped because of an increase in the
temperature of the Arctic Sea.

The loss of the sea otters has led to
an increase in the number of sea
urchins, which the otters used to eat.

FACTFILE: Endangered species

More than 1000 species of living thing are endangered worldwide. The World Conservation Union is an international organization that maintains a list of endangered plants and animals, known as the red list. Nearly a quarter of all mammal species and 12 per cent of all bird species are endangered.

Sea urchins eat a kind of seaweed called kelp that grows in the ocean all round the Aleutians, so as their numbers have increased, the kelp 'forests' have begun to disappear.

Greenpeace campaigns

In the past, Greenpeace has campaigned against the slaughter of seal pups for the fur industry, and against the unnecessary killing of dolphins when they get caught up in fishermen's drift nets. Greenpeace has also supported the ban on the trading of ivory and rhino horns, and the killing of endangered animals for their skin or meat. In more recent times Greenpeace has funded scientific research aimed at proving that global warming, toxic waste dumping and nuclear energy endanger the planet's species as well as the planet itself.

The skinned remains of this illegally hunted Siberian tiger were found in the far east of Russia. Logging of the forests where Siberian tigers live, and hunting them for their skins, have reduced the population to only about 400 animals. ▼

▲ A young protester demonstrates against genetically modified food outside the 'Good Food Show' in London, UK.

THE HUMAN ENVIRONMENT

The same processes that threaten the animal world and the planet itself threaten Earth's human population, too. As climate changes begin to affect environments, the people who depend on those environments are affected. In areas of the world such as Africa, changes in climate have brought drought, as the annual rains fail to appear and food crops die. In other parts of the world fierce storms cause major catastrophes. Even in countries with moderate climates such as Britain, changes in winter rainfall have caused minor flooding and damage.

GM foods

Another cause for concern is genetically modified (GM) foods. Scientists have found ways of altering the genetic 'blueprint' that decides how an animal or plant will develop. The aim of these alterations is to produce bigger, faster-growing food crops that are resistant to diseases. Some crops are modified to be resistant to herbicides, which makes it easier to kill invading weeds. However, it is not yet known what the effect of releasing these altered genes into the natural environment might be.

Poisonous wastes

Another threat to human life comes from toxic (poisonous) wastes, such as those from the chemical industry and from nuclear power stations. Toxic chemicals can cause serious diseases in humans, and nuclear waste can cause cancer if it escapes into the environment. Toxic chemicals have been found in animals living in very remote areas such as the Arctic and Antarctic, while recent studies around British nuclear power stations have found high levels of radioactive materials in fish and other creatures in the nearby sea.

In 1986 the world's worst nuclear disaster occurred, when a nuclear reactor exploded at Chernobyl, Ukraine. Today, many years later, there are high levels of cancer among the people of the area. Worse still would be a nuclear war. In 2002 there

was a very real threat of nuclear war between India and Pakistan. If such an event were to take place, the clouds of radioactive fallout from nuclear explosions would affect most of the planet.

▲ After the accident at Chernobyl, the damaged nuclear reactor was encased in a huge concrete slab. It is known as the Mausoleum because the dead bodies of workers are still inside.

FACTFILE: The world's nuclear powers

Seven countries are known to have nuclear weapons and have tested them. Israel is known to have nuclear weapons, but has never admitted it or tested them. Iran, Iraq, Libya and North Korea are thought to be developing nuclear weapons.

Country	No. of missiles	Max. range (kilometres)	No. of nuclear tests
USA	12,070	13,000	1,030
Russia	8,240	11,000	715
France	510	4,800	not known
China	425	11,000	45
Britain	400	12,000	45
Israel	*100	1,500	none
India	*60	3,200	5
Pakistan	*10	3,200	2

* Estimate.

◀ Air pollution from factory chimneys in New York State, USA.

CLIMATE CHANGE

Greenpeace believes that global climate change, caused by the greenhouse effect, is the greatest threat to the planet. In 1992 at the Rio de Janeiro Earth Summit, 178 countries met and agreed to reduce the emissions of carbon dioxide and other gases that cause the greenhouse effect. In 1997, at the Kyoto summit meeting in Japan, world governments agreed further plans to reduce the amount of carbon released into the atmosphere.

A small number of scientists argue that the greenhouse effect is natural and that the Earth is heating up for reasons that have nothing to do with people or pollution. They argue that countries are wasting money in seeking energy sources that do not produce greenhouse gases, such as solar and wind power, when they could instead spend the money on helping poorer countries cope with climate change. This is an argument favoured by industries that depend on fossil fuels. Some of these industries are very powerful and can influence the decisions of governments.

The role of Greenpeace

Greenpeace has campaigned to encourage governments to reduce emissions of carbon dioxide as agreed at

The Greenfreeze fridge uses refrigerating gases that do not cause global warming or damage the ozone layer. They are built at this factory in China. ▶

the Kyoto summit. It has already successfully campaigned against CFCs, the compounds that were once used in aerosols and refrigeration systems but are now banned in many countries because they damage the ozone layer. The gases used in newer fridges are less harmful but they do add to the greenhouse effect.

Greenpeace has therefore worked with Calorgas to develop an environmentally friendly alternative that uses less harmful gases such as pentane or butane as cooling agents.

Is it effective?

Greenpeace can only campaign, and encourage governments to keep to the terms of the Kyoto Treaty. The measures agreed to at Kyoto are seen by Greenpeace supporters and other environmentalists as the minimum that needs to be done to combat global warming. When US President George W. Bush announced in 2001 that the USA would not sign the treaty, it was a great blow to the Greenpeace campaign.

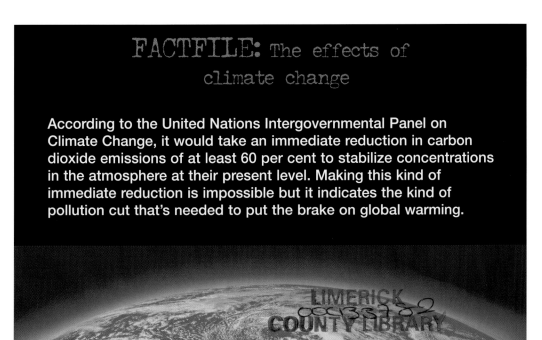

FACTFILE: The effects of climate change

According to the United Nations Intergovernmental Panel on Climate Change, it would take an immediate reduction in carbon dioxide emissions of at least 60 per cent to stabilize concentrations in the atmosphere at their present level. Making this kind of immediate reduction is impossible but it indicates the kind of pollution cut that's needed to put the brake on global warming.

fuel called Mox. But the process produces liquid waste contaminated with radioactivity, some of which is pumped into the sea. There are also worries that the plutonium in the Mox pellets could be used to make nuclear weapons, if it fell into the wrong hands.

Such campaigns include the publication of information on the movement of nuclear waste around the world and across countries. This is so that people will know if a shipment is passing through their area. However new laws, introduced in Britain after the September 11 2001 attacks in the USA, now limit the information that Greenpeace can publish about the movement of nuclear waste or the safety of nuclear power plants.

NUCLEAR POWER

Greenpeace has campaigned against nuclear weapons, nuclear power and nuclear waste since its earliest days. Its long-term goals are to persuade governments to decommission (shut down) all nuclear power stations and to end all shipments and dumping of nuclear waste. Greenpeace also encourages alternatives to nuclear power plants that are less damaging to the environment, such as wind power.

Nuclear waste

Greenpeace campaigns against the movement of nuclear waste, which in the event of an accident could cause contamination of an area with radiation. They also oppose the reprocessing of nuclear fuel. Reprocessing is a chemical operation that reclaims uranium and plutonium from used nuclear fuel, and turns them into pellets of another nuclear

Opposing 'Star Wars'

Greenpeace has also become an important voice in opposing what it sees as a threat to nuclear arms stability caused by the American government's 'Star Wars' technology. This system aims to provide a defensive ring of anti-missile systems around the USA so that any incoming nuclear or other missile can be shot down before it reaches its target. It is possible, Greenpeace claims, that if the USA had such a system it would then be under no threat from other nuclear powers and could use its own nuclear weapons without danger of retaliation. In reaction to such a possibility, other nuclear powers may try to make more effective nuclear weapons that could penetrate the Star Wars technology. The hard-won reductions in world nuclear weapons would be lost as another round of nuclear testing and bomb making began.

> "Missile Defence was supposed to complete the walls of fortress America. Today, that assumption lies in ruins, and the utter irrelevance of NMD to the real threats facing the United States has been demonstrated beyond question."
>
> Anatol Lieven, *The Times*, 13 September 2002.

Greenpeace campaigners outside the headquarters of NATO in Brussels were arrested while protesting against the US 'Star Wars' anti-nuclear missile system. ▼

▲ Greenpeace activists try and stop Japanese and Norwegian whaling ships from catching and killing whales. This Greenpeace inflatable is trying to stop a recently caught minke whale from being hauled on to a giant whaling ship.

WHALES

The problem

People have always hunted whales for their valuable oils and flesh. In 1946, fourteen countries involved in whaling, worried by falls in whale numbers, set up the International Whaling Commission (IWC), an organization that aimed to preserve whale stocks. But the IWC was ineffective, and whaling countries killed even more whales. By 1972 most whale populations were half what they had been in 1946. The United Nations called for a ten-year ban on whaling, but whaling nations were not going to give up their fleets so easily.

The role of Greenpeace

In its early days, Greenpeace took on the whaling fleets. Greenpeace vessels followed the fleets in fast inflatable boats, putting themselves between the ships and their prey. Activists filmed the killing of whales and released the films to the media. The actions of a few committed people, working with very limited funds, raised public awareness and prevented the actual killing of hundreds of whales.

Was it effective?

In 1982 the IWC agreed to a moratorium (complete ban) on all whaling, which came into effect in 1986. Greenpeace can claim responsibility for bringing the plight of whales to the world's attention. However, within two years whaling

nations were trying to lift the ban, and every year at the IWC annual meeting Japan tries to persuade members to reintroduce commercial whaling.

Despite the fact that whaling has been banned for 17 years, the numbers of some whale species have not recovered as was hoped. Scientists believe that climate change and overfishing are responsible for this.

Scientific hunting

Two countries, Japan and Norway, continue to hunt whales for scientific purposes. Greenpeace has campaigned to stop this scientific whaling and for the creation of whale sanctuaries. As well as continuing to take direct action against whalers at sea, Greenpeace also publishes information about whaling to try and persuade people, especially in Japan and Norway, that whaling should be banned. They also take part in the annual meetings of the IWC, to fight for permanent protection of whales.

FACTFILE: Whale numbers

	Before mass whaling	1986 moratorium
Blue whale	250,000	3,000
Right whale	100,000	10,000
Humpback whale	200,000	*15,000
Fin whale	550,000	120,000
Sei whale	250,000	60,000
Bowhead whale	30,000	4,000	* Estimate.

▲ Paper mills like this one at Powell River in Canada produce high levels of dioxins.

TOXIC WASTE

The problem

Many synthetic chemicals and materials are now recognized as highly toxic (poisonous) and are a danger to human health and the environment. Some of the most dangerous are dioxins, a group of chemicals that are a by-product of many industries including the manufacture of the plastic PVC (polyvinyl chloride), bleaching of paper, the manufacture of some herbicides and pesticides, and the burning of rubbish in waste incinerators. Dioxins are present in especially high quantities in major cities, especially around incinerators and factories that make plastics.

POPs

Dioxins are the most important of a group of chemicals known as POPs (persistent organic pollutants). These chemicals are persistent because they are not broken down in the body but become incorporated into the body's stored fat. An international treaty has already been put in place to eliminate these chemicals. Dioxins have been discovered in the stored fat of whales, which inhabit places far away from where POPs are manufactured. They have also been found in people living in the Arctic Circle. The release of dioxins is increasing particularly in developing countries, because companies based in the West have moved many of their factories to countries where workers can be paid less.

The role of Greenpeace

Greenpeace campaigns to bring the dangers of POPs to the world's attention, exposing businesses that are persisting in producing these chemicals. They have also campaigned against the use of waste incinerators, which release POPs into the atmosphere. Greenpeace ships measure dioxin levels in harbours and river mouths, where the chemicals have been carried downstream from factories discharging waste into rivers.

Is it effective?

Greenpeace and the other organizations opposed to the use of POPs have encouraged some big companies, such as Nike, Body Shop and Ikea, to eliminate POPs from their products. In May 2001, 91 countries signd a global treaty for the elimination of POPs. This elimination of POPs will not happen overnight,

▲ In 2000 Greenpeace activists climbed the world's tallest waste incinerator, Toshima Tower in Tokyo, Japan, to protest about the emission of dioxins from incinerators.

however, and even once their production is stopped, these chemicals will remain in the environment for many years,

FACTFILE: One small fire

Between 9 and 12 July 1997, at least 400 tonnes of PVC burned in an accidental fire at a plastics factory in Hamilton, Ontario, Canada. The factory was storing bales of PVC material. An analysis of soot and ash samples after the fire at the plant found levels of dioxin 66 times higher than those permitted even for industrial land. This one fire increased the annual dioxin emissions for the whole of Canada by 4 per cent in 1997.

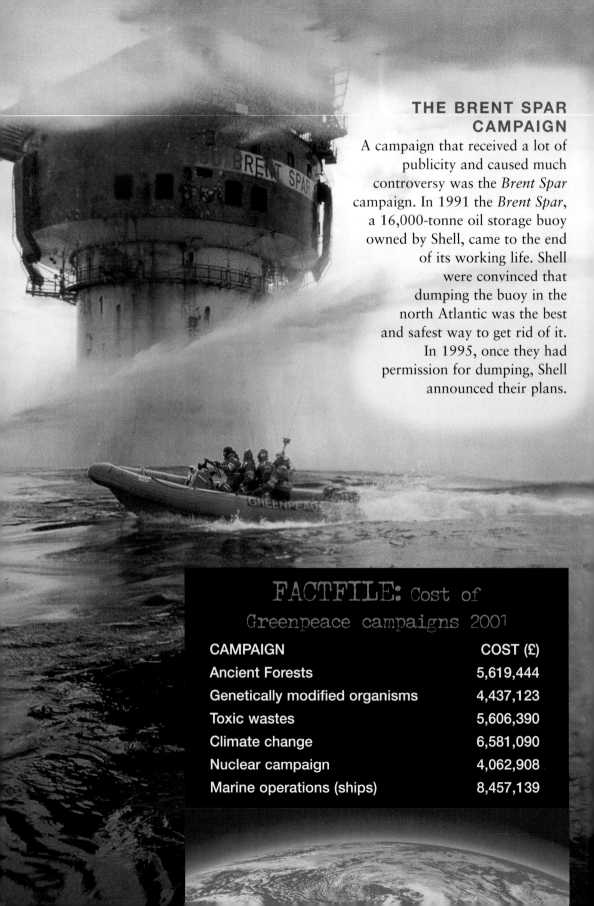

THE BRENT SPAR CAMPAIGN

A campaign that received a lot of publicity and caused much controversy was the *Brent Spar* campaign. In 1991 the *Brent Spar*, a 16,000-tonne oil storage buoy owned by Shell, came to the end of its working life. Shell were convinced that dumping the buoy in the north Atlantic was the best and safest way to get rid of it. In 1995, once they had permission for dumping, Shell announced their plans.

FACTFILE: Cost of Greenpeace campaigns 2001

CAMPAIGN	COST (£)
Ancient Forests	5,619,444
Genetically modified organisms	4,437,123
Toxic wastes	5,606,390
Climate change	6,581,090
Nuclear campaign	4,062,908
Marine operations (ships)	8,457,139

Greenpeace and other groups strongly opposed the dumping of the *Brent Spar*. They argued it was wrong to dump huge industrial structures like this at sea, and that industry should recycle and reuse materials where possible. They were also worried that oil and toxic chemicals still in the buoy could cause pollution. They thought that the *Brent Spar* should be disposed of on shore.

Occupying the platform

In April 1995 more than twenty Greenpeace activists occupied the empty *Brent Spar* platform. Greenpeace photographers and cameramen recorded the occupation and the Greenpeace vessel the *Moby Dick* stood by to ferry activists and supplies to and from the platform. Shell reacted by removing the protesters from the *Brent Spar*. They then started to tow it to a deep-sea dumping site near Scotland.

During the towing operation two more Greenpeace protesters were lowered onto the *Brent Spar* from a helicopter. Shell soaked the two new protesters with high-pressure hoses, but they did not leave. In support of the action, many people boycotted (stopped buying) Shell products.

◄ Greenpeace activists try to get close to the *Brent Spar* but are stopped by high-pressure water sprays.

Success

Greenpeace's campaign received huge publicity and was eventually successful. Shell agreed not to dump the *Brent Spar*, and it was towed into a safe harbour. But when experts examined the rig, they found that there was much less oil in its tanks than Greenpeace had estimated. Greenpeace apologized for overestimating the amount of oil, but said that it was still not acceptable to dump such material in the sea.

A mistaken campaign?

The *Brent Spar* was eventually chopped up for scrap and recycling of reusable materials, part of it being used in the building of a ferry terminal. Greenpeace saw the campaign as a success, since it led to a treaty forbidding the dumping of old oil and gas installations at sea.

Some studies made since have suggested that dumping the *Brent Spar* at sea would have been no worse for the environment than dumping it on land. Also, two marine biologists found that the *Brent Spar* had been home to large colonies of corals, and suggested that leaving such structures in place might be a good way of preserving rare corals.

With hindsight, the Greenpeace *Brent Spar* campaign may have exaggerated the buoy's danger to the environment. The campaign cost both Shell and Greenpeace a great deal of money, and some people think it was a costly mistake.

THE ANTI-FUR CAMPAIGN

The problem

In Arctic areas, seals were an important resource for native people for hundreds of years. They hunted them with simple weapons for their meat, skins and oil. But in the 20th century commercial sealing ships began hunting the young animals simply for their fur, clubbing them to death and abandoning the stripped carcasses. By the time Greenpeace began campaigning in 1976, seal numbers had fallen dangerously low.

The role of Greenpeace

Greenpeace campaigners put themselves between the endangered animals and the huge icebreaking ships that came to hunt the seals. Another tactic was to paint the seal pups' fur with harmless green dye, rendering them worthless. The campaigns attracted lots of media attention.

In 1984 Greenpeace launched another anti-hunting campaign, this time against the use of leg-hold traps used extensively in Canada to trap fur-bearing animals. This campaign was very powerful, using advertising to persuade people not to buy fur coats.

Was it effective?

Greenpeace's seal campaigning was certainly successful. All over Europe people began to turn against buying sealskin products, and sales slumped worldwide. Seal products were no longer fashionable and the commercial sealers no longer had a motive for hunting. In 1982, due to public pressure, the European Parliament banned the import of sealskins. In the Arctic, local people still hunted and sold seal products, but over-hunting of seals had stopped.

Greenpeace's anti-fur campaign also caused sales of furs to slump, but this time Greenpeace abandoned their campaign. The slump in sales had hit the Inuit people of Canada badly. They depended on trapping for their existence and Greenpeace chose the lesser of the two evils, choosing to let the issue go rather than destroy Inuit culture.

◀ The photo for Greenpeace's poster against the fur trade was taken by the internationally famous photographer David Bailey.

"[We] find a seal twenty feet before the monstrous…ice-crushing bow of the *Arctic Endeavour*. We hold our position with our backs to the ship…. The *Arctic Endeavour* plunges forward, picking up speed…. We feel her coming…the ice trembles and cracks. Blocks of chunky ice tumble forwards. The crewman on the ice screams, 'Stop 'er captain, the stupid asses ain't a moving'. The engines cut and reverse. The ship slowly grinds to a halt five feet behind our backs. I pick up the baby whitecoat [seal] and remove it to safety."

Paul Watson, a Greenpeace activist

◀ Paul Watson (left) and Robert Hunter block the path of the icebreaker *Arctic Endeavour* in their attempt to protect seal pups from being killed for their fur.

ANTARCTICA

The problem

Antarctica is a precious, unspoiled area of the world. But it also affects the global climate, because environmental changes in Antarctica cause changes around the world (see factfile).

There is evidence that there are rich deposits of oil, metals and other minerals deep under Antarctica. Since the 1950s there have been international agreements to limit scientific and industrial exploration there. But in the 1980s, governments began to discuss exploitation of Antarctica's natural resources.

The role of Greenpeace

It was at this point that Greenpeace became involved, campaigning to protect the continent from the damage that this kind of exploitation could cause. Greenpeace began to

▲ In 1997 Greenpeace sailed an icebreaker around James Ross Island near Antarctica. It was only possible to do this because for the first time global warming had melted the ice bridge connecting the island to the Antarctic mainland.

campaign for Antarctica to be given the status of a World Park (a giant nature reserve). It set up a base on James Ross Island, designed to cause as little damage as possible to the Antarctic environment. This showed how an Antarctic base could be environmetally friendly.

In 1992, after intense pressure from Greenpeace and other environmental groups, a new international agreement to protect the Antarctic environment was signed. The most important part of the agreement (known as the Madrid Protocol) was a complete ban on mining the continent for 50 years.

Was Greenpeace effective?

Greenpeace would never claim that its actions alone brought about the international agreement. But its tactics of drawing attention to what was happening and showing how an Antarctic base could be environmentally friendly contributed to the signing of the Madrid Protocol.

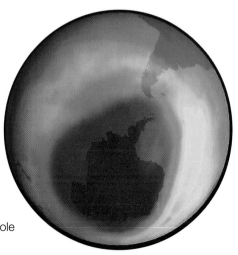

The purple area in this satellite photo is the hole in the ozone layer. On 6 September 2000 (shown here), the hole covered an area of 28 million square kilometres. ▶

FACTFILE: Antarctica

Antarctica is the last great wilderness on Earth. It lies around the South Pole and covers about 5.5 million square miles (14.2 million square kilometers). A mountain range, the Transarctic Mountains, divides it from east to west. It contains about 7 million cubic miles (30 million cubic kilometers) of ice, about 90 per cent of the world's total supply.

Antarctica has been more affected than anywhere else by damage to the ozone layer. Scientists have found that at certain times over the past 20 years, the ozone layer over Antarctica has disappeared completely.

In March 1994, the British Antarctic Survey noted the fastest sustained atmospheric warming in Antarctica since records began 130 years ago: a rise of 0.5 degrees Celsius every year since 1947. Plants that once survived only at the edges of the ice sheets have established themselves further and further south as Antarctica warms up. Along the coastline of the northern Antarctic peninsula, great ice sheets have been breaking up. The most dramatic of these was the Larsen B ice shelf (see page 45).

Scientists believe that, as Antarctic temperatures rise, the hole in the ozone layer increases due to atmospheric temperature changes.

GREENPEACE AND GOVERNMENTS

Over its 30 years of campaigning, Greenpeace has come into conflict with many of the world's governments. Some campaigns have been aimed at governments, condemning certain actions and calling for reform or for new laws and regulations. Other campaigns have targeted international industries such as the nuclear industry, and manufacturers of toxic chemicals or genetically modified crops. These industries are powerful and have a great deal of influence with the governments of the countries that they are based in. In recent times Greenpeace has taken on the US government in its anti-Star Wars campaign (see page 23).

Government attack

In 1985, agents acting on the orders of the French government planted two bombs on the Greenpeace flagship, the *Rainbow Warrior*. When the bombs went off the ship sank, and one member of the crew, Fernando Pereira, was killed. The *Rainbow Warrior* was in Auckland, on its way to draw media attention to a French nuclear test at Moruroa Atoll. The French government must have been extremely concerned about the threat from Greenpeace to consider

The sinking of the Greenpeace ship *Rainbow Warrior*. ▼

undertaking such an act. The act of sabotage was carried out by secret agents using false passports. They must have thought that they would never be caught. But they were, and the French government had finally to admit what had happened.

Just two of the large team of saboteurs were found guilty of the crime and sentenced to ten years in prison. However, both were free by 1988, less than two years later.

Persuasion and embarrassment

Greenpeace's policies towards governments have become more complex in recent years, involving both the powers of persuasion and the threat of embarrassment. Many of its fleet of ships are equipped with scientific instruments that can measure toxic damage or climate changes. In 2001 the Brazilian government, acting on proof provided by Greenpeace, seized thousands of tonnes of illegally logged mahogany

▲ In 2001 the Brazilian government seized these illegally cut mahogany logs, which had been found hidden in the rainforest. Greenpeace worked with Brazilian government officials to stop this illegal logging.

wood and banned all trade in the wood. In the same campaign, Greenpeace is taking the British government to court for allowing some of the illegally logged wood to enter British ports.

> "For over 30 years, Greenpeace has been at the cutting edge of both environmental policy development and direct action, never losing its radical message – its role in promoting social and environmental justice is vitally important."
> Caroline Lucas, MEP

◀ The Twingo Smile car, developed by Greenpeace, uses half the fuel of a normal car and has much lower exhaust emissions.

toxic chemicals or illegal logging, Greenpeace invests in developing new technologies, working with established industries to produce greener products.

Greener cars

For example, Greenpeace has worked with a Swiss company, Esoro, to produce a car with extra-low petrol consumption. The car, based on the Renault Twingo, is 80 kg lighter than the original, has less air resistance, a more efficient engine and produces fewer exhaust fumes. It uses about half the petrol of an ordinary car. Some people have criticized the project, saying that it would have been better to spend the money on developing more efficient types of public transport.

An eco-fridge

Greenpeace has also worked with the Body Shop to promote green energy. They have helped put into production in China an eco-friendly fridge, using coolants that do not damage the environment. The fridge factory provides work for Chinese people and valuable exports for its government (see page 21).

WORKING WITH COMPANIES

In its early campaigns, Greenpeace's message was usually a simple one: ban nuclear tests, for instance, or stop whaling. But today Greenpeace is much more aware of the complexities of the things it wants to change.

Campaigning on behalf of animals such as seals, kangaroos or elephants, for example, isn't just a question of shaming people into behaving the way Greenpeace wants. Whole communities may depend upon hunting animals, manufacturing chemicals, or using climate-changing fuels. In addition to its media-grabbing stunts and its work to produce evidence of the dangers of

Corporate offenders

But Greenpeace still sometimes directly condemns the actions of a company or group of companies. A campaign begun in 2001 was the Stop Esso campaign. Greenpeace believes that Esso (ExxonMobil in the USA) is the oil company with the worst attitude to global warming. Esso, says Greenpeace, denies that global warming exists and has spent millions of dollars campaigning to stop the USA signing up to the Kyoto treaty to reduce emissions of greenhouse gases. It spends no money on research to find greener alternatives to petrol and diesel-engined vehicles. In Britain, the Stop Esso campaign involves protests outside Esso stations. Esso, in its turn, responds to the Greenpeace campaigns with its own leafleting and presents an alternative account of its actions.

▲ These windsurfers in north Wales marked the launch in 2001 of Juice, a pioneering partnership between Greenpeace and NPower to offer clean electricity.

FACTFILE:Juice

Another project that Greenpeace UK has developed is the use of Juice – electricity supplied by a company that is developing wind power farms around the coast of Britain. Greenpeace encourages its supporters to get their electricity from this company, because this will increase the demand for wind-generated electricity and encourage the British government to develop more wind farms.

COMMUNITY INVOLVEMENT

Within each national organization small local groups conduct their own local campaigns on issues that Greenpeace believes it can alter. Local Greenpeace volunteers carry out leafleting campaigns, approaching people on the street seeking support and giving out information on green issues.

Local activists

Greenpeace organizes annual meetings of its local groups to discuss methods and to give training in how to work effectively for what they believe in.

Local offices, such as the London office in the UK, run regular workshops on non-violent direct action, teaching volunteers how to conduct themselves so as not to get hurt, or arrested. Local activist groups in the UK contribute about £250,000 a year to the organization. One criticism that has been levelled at Greenpeace in the USA is that it has become too centralized, focusing too much on dealing with government and less on the activities of its local branches.

Choosing the right issues

Local groups campaign on global issues such as climate change, renewable energy,

The Irish rock band U2 at a Greenpeace protest in Ireland against the nuclear reprocessing plant at Sellafield, Cumbria. Irish people are worried that radioactive waste from Sellafield is pollluting the Irish coast.

genetically modified foods, saving ancient forests and banning whaling, but they try to highlight ways in which these issues affect local people.

In the UK for example, ancient forests are a distant topic to most people, but the fumes from waste incinerators are a clear example of dioxins being released into the air, and every supermarket has genetically modified foods on its shelves. In Canada the fate of the ancient forests is a much more immediate problem and so local groups focus on that issue.

▲ In 1984 an explosion at a chemical plant in Bhopal, India released toxic chemicals that killed over 7000 people. In 2001 Greenpeace campaigners in Bhopal called on chemical industries to stop producing toxic wastes.

ORGANIZATION IN FOCUS: Fighting the incinerators

In February 2002, Greenpeace volunteers organized a headline-grabbing campaign against a local incinerator plant. The Onyx combined incinerator and power plant in south London burns over 1000 tonnes of rubbish a day, collected from homes all over south London. Much of the material collected could be recycled or turned into compost. Instead it is burnt in the incinerator, producing poisonous dioxins that are released into the atmosphere. A group of local Greenpeace activists climbed the 100-metre-high chimney, closing down operations temporarily. Another group attached themselves to the machine feeding waste into the incinerator, so preventing the incinerator getting fuel. The event brought government policies on waste management onto the front pages of national newspapers.

YOUNG GREENPEACE

Greenpeace is not just about climbing tall chimneys or facing down whaling ships. There are many ways in which young people can and do become involved in Greenpeace's campaigns. Today's children are tomorrow's parents, and they have a right to demand that their future is not threatened by global warming, polluted skies or dangerous foods.

Young people, like adults, can work for a greener future. Young people are tomorrow's voters, and they can and do write to politicians expressing their concerns. Children can also choose to buy green products, such as trainers made without producing POPs or food that has not been genetically modified. They can boycott firms that damage the environment, and they can find out how their own habits harm the environment and learn how to change them.

▲ Like the solar energy bus, this Greenpeace solar energy display attracted attention wherever it went.

Young campaigners

Although Greenpeace does not have a youth section, young people regularly take part in campaigns, helping boycott businesses that have been targeted as eco-unfriendly, such as the International Stop Esso campaign where whole families picketed Esso petrol stations around the world. Young people also help raise funds with sponsored walks and swims. In the past Greenpeace has organized a special bus which travelled around Europe demonstrating the use of solar energy so that young people could learn first-hand how they can have all the conveniences of modern life without harming the environment.

Saving forests

Another important campaign in which young people played an important part was the Kids for Forests campaign. In early 2002, children from nineteen different countries collected signatures to a petition asking world leaders to protect ancient forests. They also reorganized their classrooms to be free from endangered hardwood tree products, produced artwork for display to the public and addressed the environment ministers of their home countries. Then in April 2002, a thousand children from the same countries marched through the streets of The Hague in the Netherlands, where the International Conference on Biological Diversity was taking place. One young protester said, 'We don't want the ministers to just talk … we are here to see that they keep their promises so that there will be forests in our future.'

Involving young people

Wherever Greenpeace goes it attracts the attention of young people, who seem to realise that the environment is more important than making a profit. Campaigners on a Greenpeace ship that went to the Amazon on the Ancient Forests campaign in 2001 spent a day with local children, who explored the ship, practised their English and swam with the campaigners in the Amazon river.

▼ A thousand young people marched through the streets of The Hague in the Netherlands in 2002, as part of the Greenpeace Kids for Forests campaign. Their banners were designed to bring attention to the crisis facing ancient forests.

While there are now many organizations dedicated to protecting the environment, none has had such an effect on the world's media as Greenpeace. In getting its activities widely reported, Greenpeace has been able to reach ordinary people. Its mixture of daredevil stunts, serious campaigning, scientific study, and negotiation with governments and big business, have helped to raise the profile of environmental issues.

HIGHLIGHTING ISSUES

It may be that much of the progress that has been made on reducing greenhouse gases, protecting endangered species, cutting toxic wastes and protecting ancient forests would have happened anyway. But Greenpeace has contributed to the successes that have been achieved.

Over its 30-year history Greenpeace has found ways to focus attention on issues that governments and businesses would rather keep quiet.

In recent times Greenpeace has focused on a small number of broad issues – global warming, deforestation, toxic products and clean energy. They have often managed to shame businesses into making their products greener.

NUCLEAR TESTS AND WHALES

Some Greenpeace campaigns never seem to come to an end. Greenpeace protests against nuclear testing in the 1980s had some success, but despite the protests, testing continues. In 1995 Greenpeace sent a ship to China to protest against nuclear tests there.

◀ The director of Greenpeace USA's toxics campaign, Damu Smith, addresses a protest against PVC at Baton Rouge, USA. Preventing emissions of toxic chemicals is a major focus of Greenpeace's campaigns.

▲ Whaling protests like this one in the North Sea in 1999 have been part of Greenpeace's work since the 1970s.

In 1996 a treaty banning all nuclear tests was approved by the United Nations, but India has not yet signed the treaty, and in 1998 Greenpeace was once again actively protesting against nuclear tests there.

Whaling is another issue that never seems to go away. In 1985 it seemed as if the world had finally come to its senses over whaling, but whalers continue to find loopholes in the agreements that they can exploit.

FACTFILE: Positive changes

In its 30 years Greenpeace has contributed to many positive changes in environmental matters, from the moratorium on whaling to the control of logging in endangered forests, from establishing Antarctica as a World Park to encouraging big corporations to find green alternatives to their products. Greenpeace has produced an eco-friendlier car, eco-friendly fridges, and a solar-powered kitchen. Equally, if not more importantly, Greenpeace has educated generations of people about the needs of the environment, and has persuaded governments to modify their policies.

Thousands of people gathered in Seattle in 1999 when the World Trade Organization held a conference there. They were concerned about the power of global business corporations.

FACING THE FUTURE

Greenpeace has changed as an organization over the years. For many of its individual activists, cyberactivism has become an important part of what they do. The internet provides a forum for discussion on environmental issues and the best way to deal with them. It also gives individual activists a voice. Some have used the internet to criticize Greenpeace for making compromises with governments.

Internet campaigns have targeted particular governments with email campaigns, spreading information around the world, and activists in different countries can now communicate easily on the issues at hand.

NEW THREATS

New threats to the environment, which the early activists had no idea about, have emerged. An example is the new 'Star Wars' initiative, which threatens to start a new round of nuclear weapons building. The possibility of terrorist attacks on nuclear shipments, or on reprocessing plants such as Sellafield in the UK, have become much more real since the attacks in the USA on September 11 2001.

GREENPEACE
AND POLITICIANS
“Increasingly, politics isn't about governments and parties anyway; for many people, it's about corporate power. And while some people may be disillusioned with voting once every four years, many more are getting involved in another kind of politics – taking direct action to stop the corporations**”**.

Laura Yates, Greenpeace

In March 2002, most of the Larsen B ice shelf in the Antarctic dramatically collapsed. Over 3200 square kilometres of ice broke up into thousands of small pieces. It was one of the most dramatic demonstrations of global warming yet seen. This melting happened faster than scientists had predicted. The main worry is that thicker ice shelves on the colder main part of the continent will collapse, causing a rise in sea levels all round the world.

A WORLDWIDE ISSUE

Events such as the collapse of the Larsen B ice shelf bring environmental issues into the public spotlight. In recent years the environment has become an important issue to ordinary people worldwide, and not just among white, middle-class Westerners. Greenpeace has offices in countries such as India, China and Russia, where the lives of ordinary working people are threatened by pollution, worsening weather conditions, drought and other environmental problems. More and more, such people are turning to organizations such as Greenpeace to find a voice. Greenpeace's future lies in providing a voice for these people.

A huge crack in the Larsen B ice shelf, Antarctica. The breaking up and melting of polar ice is a symptom of global warming. ▶

activist Someone who takes action to protest against an issue.

anti-missile systems A system of defensive missiles that can be used to shoot down incoming missiles.

CFCs (chlorofluorocarbons) Chemicals used in fridges and aerosols, which have been found to damage the Earth's ozone layer.

cull To reduce the numbers of a species of animal by killing a proportion of them.

commercial whaling Hunting and killing whales for profit.

cyberactivism Taking action by sending emails to protest about issues, or joining internet newsgroups.

direct action Protesting about an issue by trying to do something about it directly. Direct action against whaling might involve trying to stop whales being killed.

drift nets Large nets, sometimes tens of kilometres long, which are suspended in the ocean and catch everything that swims into them.

ecosystem A commmunity of interdependent living things and the environment in which they live

fossil fuels Fuels such as coal, oil and natural gas, which are the remains of ancient plants or animals buried in the Earth's crust millions of years ago.

genetically modified (GM) food Plants or animals in which the genetic 'blueprint' that decides how a living thing will develop has been altered. The alterations aim to produce bigger, faster-growing or disease-resistant foods.

global warming The process by which the Earth is gradually becoming warmer, due to an increase in the amount of carbon dioxide and other 'greenhouse' gases in the upper atmosphere.

greenhouse gases Gases in the upper atmosphere that contribute to global warming.

habitat The environment in which an animal or plant lives.

industrialized countries Countries such as those in Europe, which make most of their money from manufacturing and factories rather than farms and mines.

international waste trade The dumping of toxic waste from industrialized countries in poorer nations. Poor countries are paid large amounts of money to accept such waste.

International Whaling Commission An organization set up in 1948 to monitor and control the hunting of whales.

Inuit A group of native people of the Arctic Circle in North America.

Kyoto Protocol Part of a 1997 treaty drawn up to regulate and control worldwide emissions of carbon dioxide and other greenhouse gases.

National Missile Defense The official name for Star Wars, the system of missiles which the USA plans to build to defend the country against nuclear or chemical missile attack from abroad.

ozone-depleting Gases or liquids that destroy the ozone layer in the upper atmosphere.

ozone layer The ozone layer protects the Earth from harmful ultraviolet rays from the Sun.

PVC (polyvinyl chloride) A plastic used for everyday objects such as toys, window frames, pipes, flooring and cling film.

renewable energy Energy that comes from sources that will not run out, such as water, wind or the Sun.

scientific whaling Hunting and killing whales in order to study them.

synthetic Artificial or man-made.

toxic waste Waste products of chemical processes that are poisonous.

ultraviolet radiation A kind of radiation with a slightly shorter wavelength than visible light.

whaling The hunting and killing of whales.

FURTHER READING

BOOKS FOR YOUNGER READERS
Taking Action: Greenpeace, Marion Kozak. Heinemann, 1997
Greenpeace: Organizations that Help the World, Paul Brown. New Discovery Books, 1995
Global Warming, Fred Pearce. Dorling Kindersley, 2002
Global Warming: Our Planet in Peril. Capston editors. Bridgestone, 2002

BOOKS FOR OLDER READERS
The Greenpeace Story, Michael Brown and John May. Dorling Kindersley, 1991
Making Waves The Origin and Future of Greenpeace, Jim Bohlen. Black Rose Books, 2000
Shell, Greenpeace and the Brent Spar, A G Jordan and Grant Jordan. Palgrave, 2001.
Warriors of the Rainbow: A Chronicle of the Greenpeace Movement, Robert Hunter, Henry Holt, 1979

21st Century Debates: Climate Change, Simon Scoones. Hodder Wayland, 2001
Eyewitness Guide: Arctic and Antarctic, Barbara Taylor. Dorling Kindersley, 1995

WEBSITES
www.greenpeace.org
The website of Greenpeace International, which has links to every national Greenpeace organization, a history of Greenpeace, video material and suggestions for activities.

USEFUL ADDRESSES
Greenpeace International
Keizersgracht 176, 1016 DW Amsterdam, The Netherlands. Tel: 31 20 523 62 22. Fax: 31 20 523 62 00.
e-mail: receptie@ams.greenpeace.org

Greenpeace UK
Canonbury Villas, London N1 2PN, United Kingdom. Tel: 44 020 7865 8100. Fax: 44 020 7865 8200.
e-mail: gp-info@uk.greenpeace.org

Greenpeace USA
1436 U Street, N.W., Washington, DC 20009, USA. Tel: 1 202 462 1177 Fax: 1 202 462 4507. e-mail: greenpeace.usa@wdc.greenpeace.org

SOURCES OF QUOTES
p 31: quoted in *The Greenpeace Story* (see books for older readers).

p 44: quoted in the *Guardian*, 3 Feb 2002.

INDEX